# Contents

On the move

Our body can move in many ways.

We can lift our legs up and down.

Our head nods
up and down.

**Twist
and shake**

Which parts of
your body can
you twist, turn,
wiggle, bend or
shake?

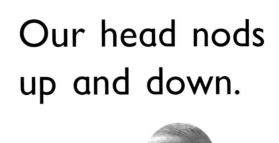

We can
make a
circle with
our arm.

How does it move?

Things around us can move, too.

A gate swings backwards and forwards.

Look and find

Look around your house. What moves up and down or round and round or backwards and forwards?

A wheel
turns round
and round.

A zip
goes up and
down.

Push it!

Many things move when we give them a push.

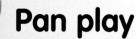

Pan play

Hold two saucepan lids in your hands. What happens if you push them together?

A door opens with a push.

We push a
wheelbarrow.

We push
a swing.

Pull it!

Many things move when we give them a pull.

Glug, glug

Fill the bathroom basin with some water. What happens if you pull the plug?

A drawer opens with a pull.

We pull
an apple off
a tree.

This tractor is pulling machinery.

Getting started

Pushes and pulls are called forces.

Get moving
Can you find three things that need a pull to move, and three that need a push?

You need a force to get things moving.

Push! The truck is moving now.

Pull!
Now the
puppet is
dancing!

Big or small

A force can be big or small.

A small push makes the ball moves slowly.

Lift off!
Find two bags. Fill one with food tins/potatoes. Which bag is easier to lift? Which needs a bigger force?

A bigger push makes the ball move faster.

It moves further too. Crash!

On the turn

You need a force to make things turn.

Pulling the wheel turns the toy car.

Pulling on the wheel steers the toy car around this corner.

Car play

Roll a toy car across the floor. Can you make it turn a corner? How?

AA 01

Slowing down

You need a force to slow things down.

Up, up and away
How would you stop a balloon from floating away?

Pull!

The dog slows down if you pull on the lead.

A push with your foot stops the ball.

Push!

We should never try to stop heavy things. They can hurt us.

Take care! Some things are just too heavy to stop!

Squash and stretch

A force
can make things
change shape.

Push!

If you sit on a bean bag,
you squash it.

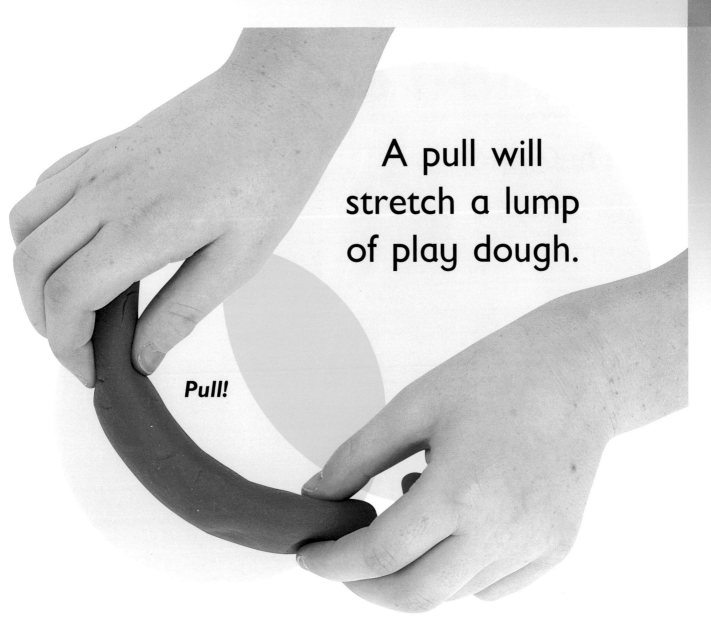

A pull will
stretch a lump
of play dough.

Pull!

Pulling and pushing make the
play dough change shape.

What a squash!

What happens when you squash a bath sponge
with your hand? What happens when you let it go?

The push of the wind

The wind
is a force.

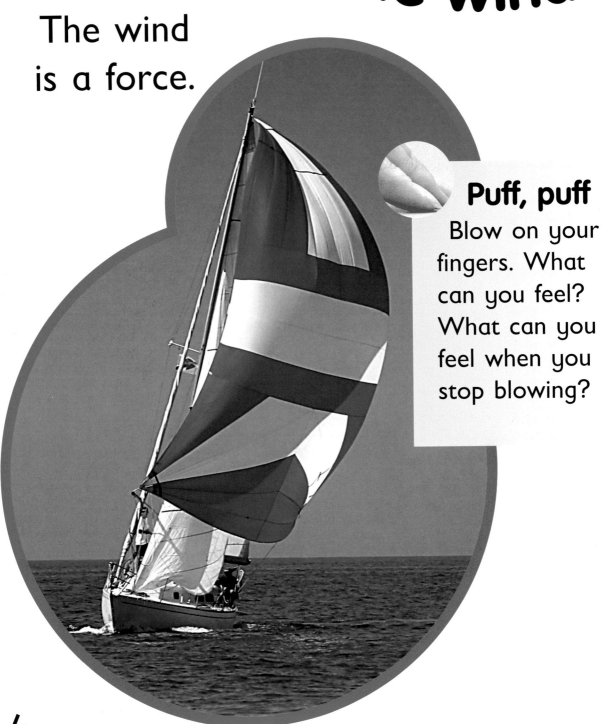

Puff, puff
Blow on your
fingers. What
can you feel?
What can you
feel when you
stop blowing?

It can push a boat over the water.

It pushes the washing on the line.

It can push a
windmill
around.

It lifts
a kite into
the air.

The force of water

Moving water
is a force.

It can push a
wheel around.

Water play

Turn on the tap – first gently, then
quickly. What changes can you hear?
What changes can you see and feel?

The river pushes
the logs along.

The sea is pushing the sandcastle down.

Glossary

Force
A push or a pull that makes something move, go faster, turn, change shape, slow down or stop.

Machine
An object made by people makes use of forces.

Machinery
Some kind of machine.

Pull
To tug something.

Push
To press something.

Squash
To make something flat by pushing on it.

Stretch
To make something long by pulling on it.

Windmill
A building or a toy with parts which turn in the wind.

Make a Plasticine snail

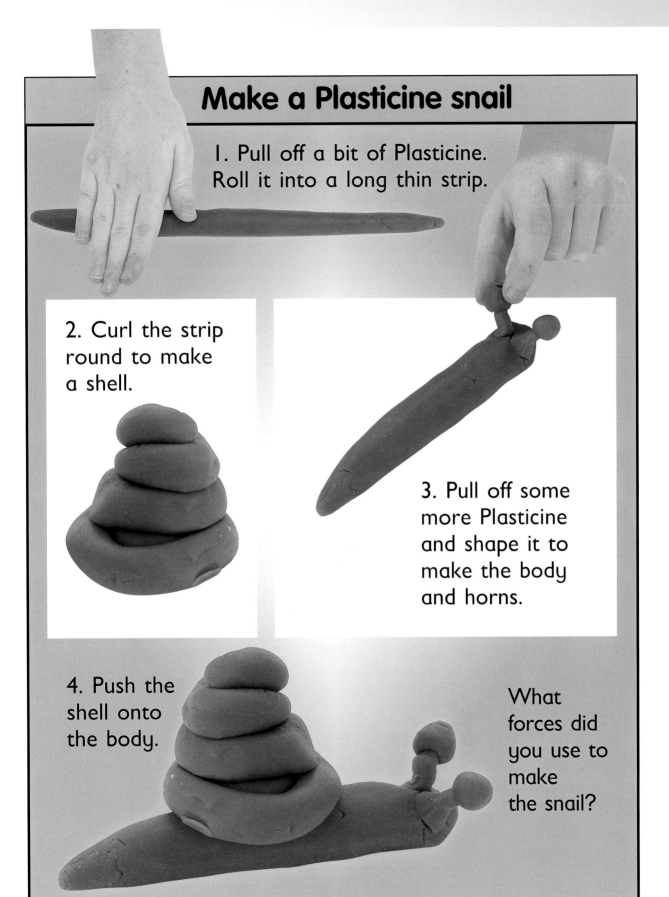

1. Pull off a bit of Plasticine. Roll it into a long thin strip.

2. Curl the strip round to make a shell.

3. Pull off some more Plasticine and shape it to make the body and horns.

4. Push the shell onto the body.

What forces did you use to make the snail?

Index